Ken Hom's
◇ Quick and Easy ◇
Cookery Course

Ken Hom is also the author of
Chinese Cookery,
Ken Hom's Vegetable and Pasta Book and
East Meets West

ADAPTED AND EDITED BY *Wendy Hobson*
ILLUSTRATIONS BY *Teresa O'Brien*

Published by William Levene Ltd
167 Imperial Drive
Harrow Middlesex
England

First published 1990
Reprinted 1991 (twice), 1992 (twice), 1993 (twice), 1994

This edition specially published by William Levene Limited
by arrangement with BBC Books
and not to be sold separately

ISBN 0 563 36125 5

CONTENTS

INTRODUCTION

*A*ll the recipes and menus in this book are designed for simplicity and rapidity of preparation. We need to be clear that 'quick and easy' entails no sacrifice of quality. It does not imply machine-made 'fast food'. It means only that the more elaborate and time-consuming recipes and menus of Chinese cookery have been omitted or re-fashioned in order to expedite the preparation of authentic and delectable meals. The essence remains the same; only the element of time has been changed.

Cooking quickly and easily comes naturally to those who spend a good deal of time in the kitchen. Of course, it is to be expected that elaborate multi-course dinners take much more time and effort. But not every meal is a major social or family event, no cook *always* has enough time, and sometimes, perhaps more often than not, a quick, easy, delectable, authentic meal is just the right thing. The preparation of such meals is what this book is about.

I have been developing these quick and easy recipes and techniques over the years, and more so of late, as my professional responsibilities have encroached upon my available kitchen time. Freshness of central ingredients remains my primary concern. I have, however, employed alternative techniques and allowed for substitution of secondary ingredients.

This has not been as difficult as it might seem. Except for a few sauces and seasonings, authentic Chinese cookery does not depend so much upon ingredients in the way, for example, that Japanese cookery does. Thus tomatoes, corn, potatoes, sweet potatoes, asparagus and a host of 'alien' foods have been readily accepted into Chinese cookery. Remember, too, that not all processed foods are to be scorned: tinned tomatoes are an excellent substitute for fresh ones, and frozen vegetables are sometimes superior to (and cheaper than) fresh but out-of-season varieties. Thus we may substitute Western or processed ingredients if necessary or desirable.

Refinements of techniques matter very much, but they too may be modified or adjusted as the food or time available permit. Pressure-cookers, electric mixers, slow-cookers, food processors and even microwave ovens have been accepted into 'authentic' Chinese kitchens. These are all time and energy savers, all perfectly acceptable to use – after all, even the wok was once an innovation.

There are very basic reasons why Chinese cookery is popular the world over: technique and a few essential seasonings can make everyone's native foods into 'Chinese'. These same virtues make for excellent 'quick and easy' food. What matters, once your pantry is stocked, is organisation, the right recipes and experience. Use this book as a point of departure. When you shop, do it when you can take your time: savour the experience of building your pantry. Note that some of the recipes have a longer list of ingredients than you might expect in a 'quick and easy' cookbook: this is essential to capture the flavours of authentic good cooking. Even 'quick and easy' food requires your attention – but there are few things in this world more worthy of your time and concern or more rewarding.

UTENSILS

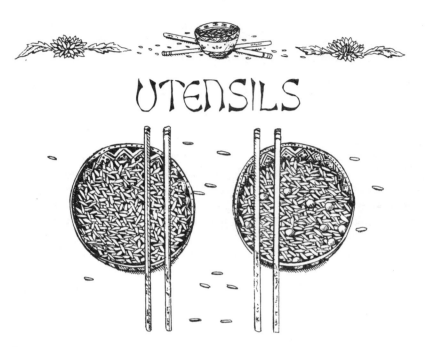

*T*he true tastes and flavours of China can only be achieved by using the appropriate cooking techniques, and proper technique requires proper equipment. While not absolutely essential for cooking Chinese food, there are a few items which will make it easier. Most are inexpensive, easily available and all are serviceable over a long period of time.

The most useful piece of equipment is the wok. It can be used for many types of cooking such as braising and deep-frying, and is particularly useful for cooking bulky vegetables like spinach, or to cook large quantities of food. It is best known, of course, as the ideal pan for stir-frying as it allows you to move the food around quickly without spilling it all over the place, and its shape spreads the heat evenly over the surface, thus making for the rapid cooking which is fundamental to stir-frying. When used for deep-frying, the smaller base of the wok requires less oil, but still provides the depth which is important to that technique.

In China most homes have round-bottomed woks which are set on top of charcoal braziers in which wood or charcoal is burnt to produce the high heat so important for Chinese cooking. The purpose of the traditional design is to concentrate intense heat at the centre, but living outside a Chinese kitchen requires some adjustment. During many years of teaching and demonstrations, I have found the most appropriate wok for a Western-type stove is one with a long wooden handle, about 12 ins (30 cm) in length and I prefer one that has a slightly flattened bottom which allows the wok to rest securely on the Western-type stoves, either electric or gas.

CHOOSING A WOK

Choose a medium-sized wok, preferably about 12 to 14 ins (30 to 35 cm) in diameter, with deep sides, a long handle and a slightly flat bottom. Some woks on the market are too shallow or too flat at the bottom, making them no better than a large frying pan or skillet. Select one which has heft to it, and if possible choose one made of carbon steel rather than of light aluminium. The latter tends to scorch and does not withstand the high temperatures required for this type of cooking. I dislike electric woks because they do not heat up to a sufficiently high temperature and tend to be too shallow to accommodate a reasonable quantity of food.

PREPARING THE WOK

Before using the wok, it is important to assemble it correctly and to clean off the manufacturer's protective coating, which will not cause you any harm but may taint the food.

To assemble the wok, first insert the hanging hook into the handle with the washers placed between the loop and the wood. Place the metal collar around the end of the handle. Push the assembled handle on to the wok and turn the hanging hook until it will no longer turn and the handle is firmly in place.

The easiest way to clean the bowl is to apply approximately two teaspoons of oil over the entire inner surface, place the wok on the stove and heat gently to soften the coating. Scrub the bowl, a scouring pad is ideal, until all the coating is removed and you have reached bare metal. The scrubbing will not damage the bowl at all.

Once clean, wash it and dry it gently on the stove to dry the bowl completely. The wok is now ready for seasoning.

SEASONING THE WOK

Rub the entire inner surface of the wok with a thick coating of corn or vegetable oil. Heat the wok gently until the oil smokes, then remove the wok from the heat and leave it until cold. Wipe off the excess oil with absorbent kitchen paper. Repeat the process two or three times. Your wok is now ready for use.

With continual use and seasoning, your wok will eventually become quite dark in colour and this will enhance the condition of the bowl. The Chinese contend that the blacker the wok the better the cook.

CLEANING THE WOK

Do not scrub a seasoned wok, just wash it in plain water without detergent. Dry it thoroughly, preferably by putting it over a low heat for a few minutes before putting it away. This should prevent the wok from rusting, but if it does, scrub off any rust with kitchen cleanser and repeat the seasoning process. If you wish to store it for a long while or if you live in a humid climate, rub the inside of the wok with a tablespoon of cooking oil for added protection before storing.

WOK ACCESSORIES

Wok stand   This is a metal ring or frame designed to keep a conventionally shaped wok steady on the burner when you are steaming, deep-frying or braising. It is useful only if you are using a round-bottomed wok, which will usually come with its own stand.

Wok lid   A wok lid is a dome-like cover, usually made from aluminium, which is used when steaming. Normally it comes with the wok, but it may be purchased separately from a Chinese or Asian market. Any large, domed pot lid which fits snugly over the wok can be used instead.

Spatula   A long-handled metal spatula, shaped rather like a small shovel, is ideal for scooping and tossing food in a wok. Any good long-handled spoon may be used instead.

BASIC CHINESE PANTRY

Quick and easy cookery is, well, quick and easy once you have at hand the basics of a Chinese pantry. These items, no longer exotic, are readily available in supermarkets and speciality food shops. And there need be very little waste involved in stocking up your store-cupboard as almost every one of these basic ingredients will keep nicely for a long time. You will have to shop only for fresh ingredients – those given in the Shopping List at the beginning of each recipe; it is assumed that, having read this section, you will already have the staples, so these are not drawn to your attention in the same way.

Remember too that if your pantry lacks an ingredient, something else can almost certainly substitute for it. Perhaps soy sauce is the only seasoning whose flavour cannot be replaced. Everything else resolves itself to a matter of taste, *your* taste. You are in command!

BEAN CURD

Bean curd is also known by its Chinese name, *dou foo* (*dofu*), or by its Japanese name, *tofu*. It has played an important part in Chinese cookery for over 1000 years because it is highly nutritious, rich in protein, and goes well with other foods. Bean curd has a distinctive texture but a bland taste. It is made from yellow soya beans which are soaked, ground, mixed with water and then cooked briefly before being solidified. It is usually sold in two forms: in a firm cake or in a soft custard-like form. It is perfect for quick and easy meals because it is so versatile, needs little cooking, and can easily be combined with other foods. It is also quite inexpensive. The soft bean curd (sometimes called silken *tofu*) is used for soups and other dishes, while the firm type is used for stir-frying, braising and deep-frying. Firm bean curd 'cakes', white in colour, are sold in many supermarkets, health food shops and Asian grocers'. They are packed in water in plastic containers and may be kept in this state in the refrigerator for up to 5 days, provided the water is changed daily. To use firm bean curd, cut the required amount into cubes or shreds using a sharp knife. Do this with care as it is delicate. It also needs to be cooked gently as too much stirring can cause it to disintegrate. This does not, however, affect its nutritional value.

BLACK BEANS

These small black soya beans, also known as salted black beans or fermented black beans, are preserved by being fermented with salt and spices. They have a distinctive, slightly salty taste and a pleasantly rich smell and are used as a seasoning, often in conjunction with garlic or fresh root ginger. This appetite-stimulating aroma can quickly transform an ordinary fast meal into something special. Black beans can be combined with a number of foods to give them a deep rich flavour. They are inexpensive and increasingly easier to obtain; I see them often in supermarkets. Although you can buy them in tins as 'black beans in salted sauce', you may also see them packed in plastic bags, and these are preferable. The beans are usually used whole or coarsely chopped. Although some recipes require you to rinse them before use, for fast cooking I never bother with this. The beans will keep indefinitely if stored in a sealed jar in the refrigerator or in a cool place.

CHINESE WHITE CABBAGE OR BOK CHOY

Chinese white cabbage, more popularly known as bok choy, has been grown in China for centuries. Although there are many varieties, the most common and best-known is the one with a long, smooth, milky-white stem and large, crinkly, dark green leaves. The size of the plant indicates how tender it is; the smaller the better, especially in summer, when the hot weather toughens the stalks. It has a light, fresh, slightly mustardy taste and requires little cooking. Bok choy cooks quickly in soup and takes only minutes to stir-fry – perfect for fast cooking. It is now widely available in supermarkets. Look for firm crisp stalks and unblemished leaves. Store it in the bottom of the refrigerator.

CHILLIES

Fresh chillies – the seed pods of the capsicum plant – are used extensively in Chinese cookery. Although a relatively new ingredient, having been introduced from the Americas about 100 years ago, the chilli has spread rapidly throughout Asia. Chillies are becoming more and more easily available in the UK in supermarkets and specialist food shops. Although seldom used in traditional Cantonese cooking, they are ideal for flavouring food. They provide colour and form when used as a garnish, and are also added, chopped, to many dishes and sauces that require fast cooking. They are available fresh, dried or ground.

Fresh chillies Fresh chillies found in China are long and usually pointed. Both red and green are available, though you might have difficulty obtaining fresh red chillies in the UK. Their taste is mildly spicy and pungent. Smaller varieties can be found, but the larger longer ones are the most widely available. Look for fresh chillies that are bright in colour, with no brown patches or black spots. Use red chillies if possible as they are generally milder than green ones, because they sweeten as they ripen.

To prepare fresh chillies, first rinse them in cold water. Then, using a small sharp knife, slit them lengthways. Remove and discard the seeds. Rinse the chillies well under cold running water and prepare them according to the instructions in the recipe. Wash your hands, knife and chopping board before preparing other foods, and be careful not to touch your eyes until you have washed your hands thoroughly with soap and water.

Dried red chillies Although dried red chillies are associated with Sichuan-inspired dishes, they add dimension to many other types of cuisine. Some are small, thin and about ½ inch (1 cm) long. They are used to season oil for stir-fried dishes, or split and used in sauces or in braised dishes. They are normally left whole or cut in half lengthways and the seeds left in. Dried chillies can be bought at most supermarkets and Asian grocers', and they will keep indefinitely in a tightly covered jar in a cool place.

Chilli bean sauce see Thick Sauces and Pastes

Chilli powder Chilli powder, made from dried red chillies, is also known as cayenne pepper. It is pungent and aromatic, ranging from hot to very hot; it is thus widely used in many spicy dishes. You can buy it in supermarkets.

COCONUT MILK

Widely used throughout Asia, coconut milk is more important than cow's milk in the cooking of the region. It has some of the properties of cow's milk: the cream rises to the top when it is left to stand; it must be stirred as it comes to the boil; and the fat is chemically closer to butterfat than to vegetable fat. Coconut milk is not the liquid inside the coconut but the liquid 'wrung' from the grated and soaked flesh. It can be bought frozen or in tins. Both are of good quality and perfect for quick and easy cooking. For the purposes of this book, I recommend the tinned coconut milk which I have found quite acceptable and which certainly involves much less work than preparing your own. Look for the brands from Thailand or Malaysia: you can find these at Asian grocers', usually sold in 14 or 15 fl oz (380 or 400 ml) tins. Be sure to shake the tin well before opening. Place any left-over coconut milk in a covered glass jar and store in the refrigerator, where it will keep for a week.

CORIANDER, CHINESE PARSLEY OR CILANTRO

Fresh coriander is one of the relatively few herbs used in Chinese cookery. It is popular throughout southern China. It looks like flat parsley but its pungent, musky, citrus-like flavour gives it a distinctive character which is unmistakable. The feathery leaves are often used as a garnish; or the herb is chopped and mixed into sauces and stuffings. You can obtain it in many supermarkets now. When buying fresh coriander, look for deep green, fresh-looking leaves. Yellow and limp leaves indicate age and should be avoided.

To store coriander, wash it in cold water, drain it thoroughly or spin dry in a salad spinner and put it in a clean plastic bag with a couple of sheets of moist kitchen paper. I learned this technique from my cooking associate, Gordon Wing, and it works wonderfully. Stored in the salad compartment of your refrigerator, it will keep for several days.

CORNFLOUR

In China and Asia many different flours and types of starch, such as waterchestnut powder, taro starch and arrowroot, are used to bind and thicken sauces and to make batter. Traditional cooks used a bean flour because it thickened faster and held longer. Cornflour can help make quick sauces that are light and which barely coat the food so that it is never swimming in thick sauce. Added to a marinade, cornflour helps it to coat the food properly and gives the finished dish a velvety texture. It also protects food during deep-frying by helping to seal in the juices and produces a crisper coating than flour. It is used as a binder for minced stuffings too. When using cornflour in a sauce, first blend it with cold water until it forms a smooth paste and add it to the sauce at the last moment. It will look milky at first, but as the sauce cooks and thickens it turns clear and shiny.

CURRY PASTE

Curry flavours have been widely adopted by Chinese cooks. However, the Chinese like to use them more in the French style, achieving the fragrant aroma of curry but avoiding the overwhelming pungent spiciness which the Indians and Thais prefer. The most frequently used curry flavouring takes the form of prepared paste in which spices are mixed with oil and chillies. It has a better taste than the powdered variety. Be sure to get the Indian curry paste, often labelled 'Madras', which is generally the best. You can find it at some supermarkets and at many Chinese grocers'. If stored in the refrigerator after opening, curry paste keeps indefinitely.

FIVE-SPICE POWDER

Five-spice powder, also known as five-flavoured powder and five-fragrance spice powder, is available from many supermarkets (in the spice section) and Chinese grocers'. In Hong Kong Chinese chefs use this traditional spice in innovative ways, such as in marinating the inside of a Peking duck. It is a brownish powder consisting of a mixture of star anise, Sichuan peppercorns, fennel, cloves and cinnamon. A good blend is pungent, fragrant, spicy and slightly sweet at the same time. The exotic fragrance it gives to a dish makes the search for a good mixture well worth the effort. Stored in a well-sealed jar it keeps indefinitely.

FUNGUS

see Mushrooms, Chinese Dried

GARLIC

The pungent flavour of garlic is part of the fabric of Chinese cuisine. It would be inconceivable to cook without its distinctive, highly aromatic smell and unique taste. It is used in numerous ways: whole, finely chopped, crushed and pickled; and in Hong Kong I have even found it smoked. Garlic is used to flavour oils as well as spicy sauces, and is often paired with other equally pungent ingredients such as spring onions, black beans, curry paste, shrimp paste or fresh root ginger. For quick and easy preparation, give the garlic clove a sharp blow with the flat side of your cleaver or knife and the peel should come off easily. Then put the required amount through a garlic press, rather than chopping it in the traditional way – this saves time and works just as well.

Select fresh garlic which is firm and heavy, the cloves preferably pinkish in colour. It should be stored in a cool, dry place, but not in the refrigerator where it can easily become mildewed or begin to sprout.

GINGER

Fresh root ginger (actually a rhizome, not a root) in traditional Cantonese cooking is as ancient, traditional and essential as the wok. It is said that ginger from Canton is the most aromatic. Like garlic it is an indispensable ingredient of Chinese cookery. Its pungent, spicy and fresh taste adds a subtle but distinctive flavour to soups, meats, fish, sauces and vegetables. Ripe ginger is golden-beige in colour with a thin dry skin which is usually peeled before the ginger is used. It varies in size from small pieces to large knobbly 'hands'. Older shrivelled ginger is used for medicinal broths. Fresh ginger can now be found at many supermarkets and most Chinese grocers' shops. Look for 'roots' which are firm, solid and unmarked, with no signs of shrivelling. If wrapped in cling film, they will keep in the refrigerator for up to two weeks. Peeled ginger stored in a glass jar and covered in rice wine or dry sherry will last for several months. This has the added benefit of producing a flavoured wine that can be used in cooking.

Young ginger sometimes makes its appearance in Chinese grocers' shops. It is hard to find but well worth the search. Knobbly in shape and pink in colour, looking rather unformed, it is the newest spring growth of the plant. Young ginger is usually stir-fried as part of a recipe; in China it is commonly pickled. Because it is young and tender it does not need peeling and can be eaten as a vegetable. A popular way to eat pickled young ginger is with preserved 'thousand-year-old' duck eggs as a snack; it is also often served as an hors d'oeuvre.

MANGE-TOUT

This familiar vegetable combines a tender crisp texture and a sweet fresh flavour and cooks quickly. It is perhaps best when simply stir-fried with a little oil and salt and pieces of garlic and ginger. Frequently mange-tout are combined with meats. They are readily available from supermarkets and many greengrocers. Look for pods that are firm with very small peas, which means they are tender and young. They keep for at least a week, loosely wrapped, in the salad compartment of the refrigerator.

MUSHROOMS, CHINESE DRIED

There are many grades of these wonderful mushrooms said to have been produced for more than 1000 years in southern China. Black or brown in colour, they add a particular flavour and aroma to Chinese dishes. The best are very large ones with a lighter colour and a highly cracked surface; they are usually the most expensive. As you may imagine, they are very popular in Chinese cookery. Dried food shops in China carry all grades heaped in mounds, with the more expensive grades elaborately boxed. Outside China they can be bought from Chinese grocers' in boxes or plastic bags. Chinese dried mushrooms are expensive but a little goes a long way. Keep them stored in an air-tight jar in a cool dry place. Fresh ones (popularly known as Shiitake mushrooms – a Japanese term) are not an adequate substitute; the Chinese never use them fresh, preferring their distinct, robust, smoky flavour and yielding texture when dried. They are used chopped and combined with meats, fish and shellfish. They are well worth the relatively short time it takes to prepare them as they add a rich flavour to food.

To use Chinese dried mushrooms, soak the mushrooms in a bowl of warm water for about 20 minutes or until they are soft and pliable. Squeeze out the excess water and cut off and discard the woody stems. Only the caps are used.

The soaking water can be saved and used in soups or for cooking rice. Strain through a fine sieve to discard any sand or residue from the dried mushrooms. Dried mushrooms are particularly useful if you are in a hurry and do not have time to make a stock. Their presence will cover a multitude of omissions.

NOODLES/PASTA

In China you will see people eating noodles of all kinds, day and night, in restaurants and at food stalls. They provide a nutritious, quick, light snack and are usually of good quality. There are several styles of noodles which are ideal for quick and easy cooking – for example, the fresh thin egg noodles which are browned on both sides. Thin rice noodles are much savoured also, as are the fresh ones which are readily available in Chinese grocers' shops. Below is a list of the major types of noodles (or pasta) that can be bought in this country.

Wheat noodles and egg noodles These are made from hard or soft wheat flour and water. If egg has been added, the noodles are usually labelled 'egg noodles'. They can be bought dried or fresh from Chinese grocers', many supermarkets and delicatessens. Flat noodles are usually used in soups and rounded noodles are best for stir-frying or pan-frying. The fresh ones can be frozen successfully if they are first well wrapped. Thaw them thoroughly before using.

Wheat and egg noodles are very good blanched and served with a main dish instead of plain rice. Dried wheat or fresh egg noodles are best. Allow 4 oz (110 g) fresh or dried Chinese egg or wheat noodles per person. To prepare fresh noodles, immerse them in a pan of boiling water and cook for 3–5 minutes or until done to your taste. To prepare dried noodles, cook either according to the instructions on the packet or in boiling water for 4–5 minutes. Then drain and serve.

If you are cooking noodles some time in advance of serving them or before stir-frying them, toss the cooked drained noodles in 2 teaspoons sesame oil and put them into a bowl. Cover this with cling film and refrigerate. The cooked noodles will remain useable for about 2 hours.

Rice noodles Rice noodles are popular in southern China. I find them a great convenience as, being dried, they do not need refrigeration and are quickly prepared for a fast meal. They are available from Chinese grocers' and are sometimes called 'rice stick noodles'. They are flat and about the length of a chopstick. They can also vary in thickness: use the type called for in the recipe. Rice noodles are very easy to use and inexpensive. Simply soak them in warm water for 20 minutes or until they are soft. Drain them in a colander or sieve and then use in soups or stir-fried dishes.

Bean thread (transparent) noodles These, also called cellophane noodles, are made not from a grain flour but from ground mung beans. They are available dried, and are very fine and white. Easy to recognise, packed in their neat plastic-wrapped bundles, they are stocked by most Chinese grocers' and some supermarkets. They are never served on their own, but are added to soups or braised dishes or are deep-fried and used as a garnish – they are suitable for a quick meal. They must be soaked in warm water for about 5 minutes before use. As they are rather long, you might find it easier to cut them into shorter lengths after soaking. If you intend to fry them, they need first to be separated. They are quite brittle so a good technique is to separate the strands within a large paper bag to keep them from flying all over the place. If you are going to fry them, do not soak them before use.

Oils

Oil is the most commonly used cooking medium in Chinese cuisine and the favourite is groundnut (peanut) oil. Animal fats, usually lard and chicken fat, are also used in some areas. I prefer to cook with groundnut oil as I find animal fats in general too heavy.

Oil can often be re-used after frying. When this is possible, simply allow the oil to cool after use and filter it through cheesecloth or a fine-meshed sieve into a jar. Cover it tightly and store in a cool dry place. If you keep it in the refrigerator it will become cloudy but it will clarify again when it returns to room temperature. From the point of view of flavour I find that it is best to re-use oil no more than once, and this is healthier since constantly re-used oils increase in saturated fat content. However, for real clarity of flavour I prefer *not* to re-use oil at all; I think that oil should be *always* fresh as this helps achieve consistently high-quality results in cooking.

Groundnut oil Also known as peanut oil, this is the preferred oil in Chinese cookery because it has a pleasant, mild, unobtrusive taste. Its ability to be heated to a high temperature without burning makes it perfect for stir-frying and deep-frying. The groundnut oils found in China are cold-pressed and have the fragrance of freshly roasted peanuts. Some Chinese supermarkets stock the Hong Kong brands, labelled in Chinese only; these are well worth searching for. But if you cannot find them, use groundnut oil from your local supermarket.

Corn oil Corn oil is a healthful, mostly polyunsaturated oil that is good for cooking, particularly deep-frying, as it can be heated to a high temperature without burning. However, I find it rather heavy with a noticeable smell and taste.

Other vegetable oils Some of the cheaper vegetable oils available include soya bean, safflower and sunflower. They are light in colour and taste and can also be used in cooking.

Sesame Oil This thick, rich, golden-brown or dark-coloured oil is made from roasted sesame seeds, and has a distinctive nutty flavour and aroma. It is widely used in Chinese cooking in limited amounts in marinades or as a final seasoning – it is added at the end of cooking to enrich a dish subtly without overcoming its basic flavour. It is not normally used as a cooking oil with other oils except in northern China. It is sold in bottles by many supermarkets and Chinese grocers'.

OYSTER SAUCE

This is one of my favourite sauces for quick cooking. It is easy to make a delicious sauce in no time at all using oyster sauce, which gives a rich aroma to a dish. Thick and brown, it is made from a concentrate of oysters cooked in soy sauce, seasonings and brine. Despite its name, oyster sauce does not taste fishy. It has a rich flavour and is used not only in cooking but also as a condiment, diluted with a little oil, for vegetables, poultry or meat; it is very versatile. It is usually sold in bottles and can be bought in Chinese grocers' shops and some supermarkets. Look for the most expensive brands as they are the highest in quality. Keep refrigerated after opening.

RICE

Long-grain rice This is the most popular rice for cooking in southern China. The Chinese go through the ritual of washing it, but in the case of rice purchased at a supermarket, this step can be omitted for quick cookery. One of my favourite rices is the long-grain variety from Thailand which has a pleasing fragrance, like that of the Indian basmati rice. Thai aromatic long-grain rice is now available from many Chinese and Southeast Asian grocers'.

Short-grain rice Short-grain rice is not as frequently used in Chinese cooking as the long-grain type except for making morning rice porridge. It is more popular in Japan. Suitable brands which can be found in many Chinese or Japanese food shops are known as 'American Rose' or 'Japanese Rose'. Short-grain rice is slightly stickier than long-grain white rice.

RICE WINE, CHINESE

An important contributor to the flavour of Chinese cuisine, this wine is used extensively for cooking and drinking throughout the country. There are many varieties but the finest is believed to be that from Shaoxing in Zhejiang Province in eastern China. It is made from glutinous rice, yeast and spring water. Chefs frequently use rice wine not only for cooking but also in marinades. It is now readily available from Chinese grocers' and some wine merchants. Store it, tightly corked, at room temperature. A good-quality, pale, dry sherry can be substituted for Chinese rice wine but cannot equal its rich mellow taste. Do not confuse this wine with *sake*, which is the Japanese version of rice wine and quite different. Western grape wines are not an adequate substitute either.

THICK SAUCES AND PASTES

Quick and easy Chinese cookery involves the use of a number of thick tasty sauces and pastes. These are essential to the authentic taste of the food and it is well worth making the effort to obtain them. Most are now easy to find; they are sold in bottles or tins by Chinese food shops and some supermarkets. Tinned sauces, once opened, should be transferred to screw-top glass jars and kept in the refrigerator where they will last indefinitely. Using these sauces in your cooking produces delicious results with little effort.

Bean sauce This thick, spicy, aromatic sauce is made with yellow beans, flour and salt which are fermented together. It is quite salty but adds a distinctive flavour to sauces and is frequently used in Chinese cookery. There are two forms: whole beans in a thick sauce; and mashed or puréed beans (sold as 'crushed yellow bean sauce'). I prefer the whole bean variety because it is slightly less salty and has a better texture. It keeps indefinitely in the refrigerator.

Chilli bean sauce This thick, dark sauce or paste, made from soya beans, chillies and other seasonings, is very hot and spicy. Formerly used in cooking only in western China, it is now widely used throughout the country and is usually available here in jars. Be sure to seal the jar tightly after use and store in the refrigerator. Do not confuse chilli bean sauce with chilli sauce which is hot, red, thinner and made without beans and is used mainly as a dipping sauce for cooked dishes. There are Southeast Asian versions of chilli bean sauce (called *sate* sauce) which I find very spicy and hot. You can use them as a substitute for chilli bean sauce if you like really spicy food.

Hoisin sauce Widely used in this book, this thick, dark, brownish red sauce is made from soya beans, vinegar, sugar, spices and other flavourings. Sweet and spicy, it is a very popular ingredient in southern Chinese cookery. In the West it is often used as a sauce for Peking duck instead of the traditional sweet bean sauce. Hoisin sauce (sometimes also labelled 'barbecue sauce') is sold in tins and jars. When refrigerated, it keeps indefinitely.

Sesame paste This rich, thick, creamy brown paste is made from roasted sesame seeds, unlike the Middle Eastern *tahini*. It is sold in jars by Chinese food shops. If oil has separated from the paste in the jar, empty the contents into a blender or food processor and mix well. Chinese sesame paste is used in both hot and cold dishes and is particularly popular in northern and western China. If you cannot obtain it, use a smooth peanut butter instead.

SHALLOTS

Shallots are mild-flavoured members of the onion family. They are small – about the size of pickling onions – with copper-red skins and should be peeled before use just like onions. They have a distinctive onion taste without being as strong or overpowering as ordinary onions, and I think they are an excellent substitute for Chinese shallots which can sometimes be bought from Chinese grocers'. Buy shallots at supermarkets and keep them in a cool dry place (not the refrigerator).

SOY SAUCES

Soy sauce is an essential ingredient in Chinese cooking. It is made from a mixture of soya beans, flour and water which is then naturally fermented and aged for some months. The distilled liquid is soy sauce. New versions containing less salt are now available. There are two main types:

Light soy sauce As the name implies, this is light in colour, but it is full of flavour and is the best one to use for cooking. It is saltier than dark soy sauce. It is known in Chinese grocers' shops as Superior Soy. This type of soy sauce was used extensively for testing the recipes in this book.

Dark soy sauce This sauce is aged for much longer than light soy sauce, hence its darker, almost black colour. It is slightly thicker and stronger than light soy sauce and is more suitable for stews. I prefer it to light soy as a dipping sauce. It is known in Chinese grocers' shops as Soy Superior Sauce, and although used less frequently it is nevertheless important to have on hand.

SUGAR

Sugar has, appropriately, been used sparingly in the cooking of savoury dishes in China for 1000 years. Properly employed, it helps balance the various flavours of sauces and other dishes. Chinese sugar comes in several forms: as rock or yellow lump sugar, as brown sugar slabs, and as maltose or malt sugar. I particularly like to use rock sugar which is rich and has a more subtle flavour than that of refined granulated sugar. It also gives a good lustre or glaze to braised dishes and sauces. You can buy it in Chinese food shops, where it is usually sold in packets. You may need to break the lumps into smaller pieces with a wooden mallet or rolling pin. If you cannot find it, use white sugar or coffee sugar crystals (the amber, chunky kind) instead. For fast cooking, use white granulated sugar.

VINEGARS

Vinegars are widely used in China as dipping sauces as well as for cooking. Unlike Western vinegars, they are usually made from rice. There are many varieties, ranging in flavour from the spicy and slightly tart to the sweet and pungent. Experiment with them. They keep indefinitely.

White rice vinegar White rice vinegar is clear and mild in flavour. It has a faint taste of glutinous rice and is used for sweet and sour dishes.

1

FISH & SEAFOOD

*F*ish and shellfish by their very nature are best when not overcooked. The sweet succulent sea flavours are retained through careful and quick cooking. Fish is thus most appropriate for the 'quick and easy' approach. First you must buy the freshest you can find; then you must cook it quickly and with the appropriate seasonings. I think that no other cuisine matches that of the Chinese in its ability to capture the best flavours and textures of the harvest of the sea. I draw upon that heritage for the recipes in this section.

Firm white fish such as cod, haddock and even plaice lend themselves best to the steaming technique. This delicate process gently brings out the virtues of the food. Chinese spices, such as black beans, can be used on more assertively flavoured fish and shellfish such as salmon and mussels. Ginger, garlic and spring onions are very congenial seasonings for all fish or seafood. Serve any of the following recipes with another vegetable dish and rice or potatoes and you have the best of contemporary dining, whether for entertaining a large party or for informal eating with family and friends.

QUICK PAN-FRIED FIVE-SPICE FISH

On the way home from work, my widowed mother would often pick up a small whole fish or some fillets and quickly put together this nutritious meal. With stir-fried vegetables, yesterday's rice re-heated and perhaps a Western touch of salad, you have a quick, wholesome and satisfying meal. The fish also goes wonderfully well with pasta. For a more elegant meal try substituting fresh uncooked prawns for the fish.

SHOPPING LIST
  *1 lb (450 g) fresh fish fillets
    (preferably cod or haddock)*
  Garlic
  Fresh root ginger

PREPARATION TIME *10 minutes*

COOKING TIME *10 minutes*

SERVES 4

1 lb (450 g) fresh fish fillets
1 teaspoon five-spice powder
1 teaspoon salt
1½ tablespoons oil (preferably groundnut)
2 tablespoons coarsely chopped garlic
2 tablespoons coarsely chopped fresh root ginger
1½ tablespoons Chinese rice wine or dry sherry
2 teaspoons light soy sauce
2 teaspoons sesame oil

Rub the fish fillets with the five-spice powder and salt.

Heat a wok or large frying-pan until it is hot, then add the oil. Gently pan-fry the fish on each side until it is lightly browned and remove with a spatula. To the remaining oil add the garlic, ginger, rice wine, soy sauce and sesame oil. Return the fish to the wok and gently re-heat. Serve at once.

FRIED FISH WITH WHOLE GARLIC

Lovers of the 'stinking rose' – and who is not? – understand that whole garlic cloves are among the most delicious and sweetly pungent foods in the world. Garlic adds great dimension to so many different dishes, and to fish in particular. In Shanghai a dish featuring eels and whole garlic is very popular. I have adapted the recipe to use commonly available fish fillets; these work as well and are easy to prepare. If you prefer you can also substitute whole shallots or small onions for the garlic. Serve this dish with rice and stir-fried vegetables for a healthy and very tasty meal.

SHOPPING LIST
  1 lb (450 g) fresh fish fillets
    (preferably cod or haddock)
  Garlic
  Fresh root ginger

PREPARATION TIME *15 minutes*

COOKING TIME *10 minutes*

SERVES 4

    1 lb (450 g) fresh fish fillets
    1 teaspoon salt
    3 tablespoons cornflour

4 tablespoons oil (preferably
  groundnut)
8 cloves garlic, peeled
2 tablespoons coarsely chopped
  fresh root ginger

For the sauce
1 tablespoon Chinese rice wine
  or dry sherry
3 tablespoons water
1 tablespoon light soy sauce
1 tablespoon bean sauce
1 teaspoon sugar
1 tablespoon dark soy sauce

Rub the fish fillets with the salt and cornflour.

Heat a wok or large frying-pan, then add the oil. Fry the fish on both sides until it is golden-brown. Remove the fish and drain on kitchen paper.

Drain all but 1 tablespoon of oil from the pan, add the garlic and ginger and stir-fry for 20 seconds. Then add the sauce ingredients and cook for 3 minutes or until the garlic is tender. Return the fish to the wok and re-heat it. Serve at once with the garlic cloves.

STEAMED SALMON WITH BLACK BEAN SAUCE

*F*resh salmon is a luxury but every serious diner deserves it once in a while. Buy it in season when it is least expensive. Prepare it using this Chinese steaming method: it preserves all the noble characteristics of the salmon. Here I serve it with a traditional black bean sauce. It has a very pleasantly pungent taste that actually enhances the distinctive salmon flavour, making a wonderful contrast on the palate. Haddock or cod fillets make a successful substitute for salmon, or you could even try scallops.

SHOPPING LIST
> *1 lb (450 g) fresh salmon fillets,*
> *1 inch (2.5 cm) thick*
> *Garlic*
> *Fresh root ginger*
> *Spring onions*

PREPARATION TIME *10 minutes*

COOKING TIME *10 minutes*

SERVES 4–6

1 lb (450 g) fresh salmon fillets, 1 inch (2.5 cm) thick
1 teaspoon salt
2 teaspoons sesame oil
1 tablespoon oil (preferably groundnut)
2 tablespoons coarsely chopped black beans
1½ tablespoons coarsely chopped garlic
1 tablespoon finely chopped fresh root ginger
3 tablespoons coarsely chopped spring onions
1 tablespoon dark soy sauce
2 teaspoons light soy sauce
5 fl oz (150 ml) water
1 teaspoon cornflour mixed with 1 teaspoon water

Set a rack into a wok or deep pan. Put in water to a depth of 2½ inches (6 cm) and bring it to a simmer.

Rub the salmon fillets with the salt and sesame oil and place on a heatproof plate that will fit into the wok or pan. Place the plate holding the fish on the rack, cover tightly and steam for about 6 minutes. It is best to undercook the salmon slightly as it continues to cook even after it has been removed from the steamer.

While the salmon is steaming, heat a wok or large frying-pan, then add the oil, black beans, garlic and ginger. Stir-fry the mixture for 1 minute, then add the spring onions, soy sauces and water and simmer for 1 minute. Add the cornflour mixture and stir the sauce until it thickens.

When the salmon is cooked, pour the hot sauce over it and serve at once.

MUSSELS IN BLACK BEAN SAUCE

*M*ussels are an ideal 'quick and easy' food. Once they have been scrubbed clean in cold water to remove all sand, they cook very rapidly, announcing that they are done by cordially opening their shells. Make sure that they are all firmly closed before cooking: throw away any that do not close up when touched or that have damaged shells.

A greater quantity of this dish can easily be prepared for larger gatherings. I prefer to use smaller mussels; if you have a choice, try them.

SHOPPING LIST
Garlic
Fresh root ginger
3 lb (1.4 kg) fresh mussels
Spring onions

PREPARATION TIME *20 minutes*

COOKING TIME *8–12 minutes*

SERVES 4–6

2 tablespoons oil (preferably groundnut)
4 tablespoons coarsely chopped black beans
3 tablespoons coarsely chopped garlic
2 tablespoons coarsely chopped fresh root ginger
3 lb (1.4 kg) fresh mussels, well scrubbed
2 tablespoons coarsely chopped spring onions
2 teaspoons light soy sauce

Heat a wok or large frying-pan, then add the oil, black beans, garlic and ginger. Stir-fry for 20 seconds and add the mussels. Continue to cook for 5 minutes or until all the mussels have opened. Discard any which have difficulty opening or do not open at all. Add the spring onions and soy sauce. Give the mixture a final stir and serve at once.

STIR-FRIED PEPPERS WITH SCALLOPS

Scallops are fragile, sweetly delicate morsels and need very little preparation or cooking time. They embody all the qualities aimed for in this book, being quick, easy and delicious. In this recipe I combine them with nutritious, tasty and colourful red and green peppers. The result is a festive-looking dish that belies its ease of preparation: perfect for a family meal or as the centrepiece of a dinner party prepared at short notice.

Mussels or clams may be substituted for the scallops and asparagus, courgettes or mange-tout for the peppers. If you like spicy food, add 2 finely sliced fresh chillies.

SHOPPING LIST
> *1 lb (450 g) fresh scallops*
> *8 oz (225 g) red peppers*
> *4 oz (110 g) green pepper*
> *Spring onions*
> *Garlic*
> *Fresh root ginger*

PREPARATION TIME *15 minutes*

COOKING TIME *8 minutes*

SERVES 4–6

1 lb (450 g) fresh scallops
8 oz (225 g) red peppers
4 oz (110 g) green pepper

1½ tablespoons oil (preferably groundnut)
1½ tablespoons coarsely chopped spring onions
1 tablespoon coarsely chopped garlic
2 teaspoons finely chopped fresh root ginger

For the sauce
1 tablespoon light soy sauce
2 teaspoons yellow bean sauce
2 tablespoons Chinese rice wine or dry sherry
1 teaspoon sugar
1 teaspoon sesame oil

Wash the scallops, pat them dry with kitchen paper and set them aside. De-seed the peppers and cut them into 1 inch (2.5 cm) squares.

Heat a wok or large frying-pan and add the oil, spring onions, garlic and ginger, and stir-fry for 10 seconds. Then add the peppers and stir-fry for 2 minutes. Stir in the scallops and the sauce ingredients. Continue to cook for another 4 minutes. Serve at once.

CRISPY PRAWNS

During one of my many trips to Australia, Charmaine Solomon, an authority on Asian cuisines, introduced me to this dish. It is to be found in one of her delightfully written cookbooks and I unabashedly lift it and share it with you. The prawns are so good that they could serve as a main course, and they are so tasty that no dipping sauce is needed.

SHOPPING LIST
> *1 lb (450 g) fresh uncooked*
> *prawns*
> *Breadcrumbs*

PREPARATION TIME *25 minutes*

COOKING TIME *3–4 minutes*

SERVES 6–8 as a starter

1 lb (450 g) fresh uncooked
prawns

2 teaspoons light soy sauce
1 tablespoon Chinese rice wine
or dry sherry
1 teaspoon five-spice powder
¼ teaspoon freshly ground
black pepper
15 fl oz (400 ml) oil (preferably
groundnut)
8 tablespoons cornflour
2 eggs, beaten
10 tablespoons breadcrumbs

Peel the prawns and discard the shells. Using a small sharp knife, partially split the prawns lengthways and remove the fine digestive cord – you can omit this stage. Pat the prawns dry with kitchen paper. Mix the prawns with the soy sauce, rice wine, five-spice powder and pepper.

Heat a wok or large deep frying-pan, then add the oil. While the oil is heating, dip the prawns in the cornflour, shaking them gently to remove any excess, then dip them into the beaten eggs and finally coat them thoroughly with the breadcrumbs. A clean and easy way to do this is to place the cornflour and the breadcrumbs in two separate polythene or paper bags. Toss the prawns gently in the first bag with the cornflour, remove them and put them in the bowl with the beaten eggs, making sure that they are well coated. Then transfer them with a slotted spoon to the bag containing the breadcrumbs and toss gently.

When the oil begins to smoke slightly, deep-fry the coated prawns for 3–4 minutes or until they are golden-brown. Drain them well on kitchen paper and serve at once.

Prawns in Ginger Sauce

Again, one of my quick and easy favourites, prawns – this time with a zesty ginger sauce to make a spicy and refreshing treat. This delightful and visually attractive dish can be served over rice for a one-dish meal that will satisfy both the stomach and the palate. It can also double as a starter for a dinner party.

Shopping List
1 lb (450 g) fresh uncooked prawns
Fresh root ginger
Fresh coriander

Preparation Time *20 minutes*

Cooking Time *4 minutes*

Serves 4

1 lb (450 g) fresh uncooked prawns
1 teaspoon salt
1 teaspoon cornflour
1 teaspoon sesame oil
1½ tablespoons oil (preferably groundnut)
3 tablespoons finely chopped fresh root ginger

For the sauce
2 tablespoons Chinese rice wine or dry sherry
1 tablespoon light soy sauce
1 tablespoon water
½ teaspoon salt
1 teaspoon sugar
2 tablespoons finely chopped fresh coriander
2 teaspoons sesame oil

Peel the prawns and discard the shells. Using a small sharp knife, partially split the prawns lengthways and remove the fine digestive cord – if you are particularly short of time you can omit this stage. Pat the prawns dry with kitchen paper and combine them with the salt, cornflour and 1 teaspoon sesame oil.

Heat a wok or large frying-pan, then add the oil, prawns and ginger. Stir-fry the mixture for 30 seconds. Then add the sauce ingredients and continue to cook for 2 minutes. Serve at once.

HOT PEPPER PRAWNS

I was introduced to this dish one evening when I dined with Madhur Jaffrey and her husband at the Shun Lee Palace restaurant in New York. She suggested that I try it, predicting that I would appreciate the imaginative interplay of pungent aromas and spicy flavours. How right she was. This is an exciting treat for the tastebuds and very easy to prepare. Serve it with rice. For a one-dish meal double the quantity of sauce and toss sauce and prawns with fresh egg noodles or rice noodles.

SHOPPING LIST
  1 lb (450 g) fresh uncooked
    prawns
  2 fresh chillies
  Garlic
  Spring onions

PREPARATION TIME *18 minutes*

COOKING TIME *4 minutes*

SERVES 4

  1 lb (450 g) fresh uncooked
    prawns
  1 teaspoon salt
  2 teaspoons cornflour

2 teaspoons sesame oil
2 tablespoons oil (preferably
  groundnut)
2 fresh chillies, de-seeded and
  coarsely chopped
1 tablespoon black beans
2 tablespoons coarsely chopped
  garlic
4 tablespoons coarsely chopped
  spring onions
3 tablespoons white rice vinegar
2 tablespoons dark soy sauce
1 tablespoon sugar
2 teaspoons cornflour mixed
  with 2 teaspoons water

Peel the prawns and discard the shells. Using a small sharp knife, partially split the prawns lengthways and remove the fine digestive cord – if time is short, omit this stage. Pat the prawns dry with kitchen paper and combine with the salt, cornflour and sesame oil and mix well.

Heat a wok or large frying-pan and add the oil and prawns. Stir-fry for 1 minute, then remove the prawns with a slotted spoon. To the remaining oil add the chillies, black beans, garlic and spring onions. Stir-fry for 20 seconds and add the vinegar, soy sauce and sugar. Stir in the cornflour mixture and return the prawns to the wok. Cook for another 2 minutes and serve at once.

2

POULTRY

*C*hicken, duck, pigeon, pheasant and quail: poultry in its many forms has been central to the Chinese cuisine for millennia. And the Chinese, in my opinion, are the world's experts in cooking poultry. All parts of each bird are used and, after cooking has transformed them, prized: the wings, the entrails, even the feet!

In the West we do not have such a wide variety of poultry so easily available and many of the game birds require extensive preparation not appropriate to the 'quick and easy' approach. Thus here I stay with what I have elsewhere called 'the sweet bird of our youth' – chicken. Of all poultry it is the most accessible and adaptable. It is relatively inexpensive, easy to cook and goes well with almost every other food. With its own delicate taste and great receptivity to other flavours, it lends itself to many recipes. Here I use parts of the chicken that are easy to cook, such as breasts and wings. Where longer cooking is required or expedient, I use chicken thighs. I have also included a few turkey recipes here – turkey is another nutritious and versatile food and deserves a bigger place in our diet.

STIR-FRIED SMOKED CHICKEN WITH CHINESE LEAVES

Smoked chicken and duck are very popular in China. Such delicacies require a time-consuming process of smoking that, fortunately, is done for us. Smoked chicken and duck are readily available in supermarkets and speciality food shops. Thus we can turn a complex recipe into something quick and easy as in this dish, a north Chinese favourite, easy to make and very pleasing to the eye and the palate. Courgettes, mange-tout, peppers or carrots may be used instead of Chinese leaves. With rice and a salad the dish makes a substantial and nutritious meal.

SHOPPING LIST
  1½ lb (700 g) smoked chicken
  1 lb (450 g) Chinese leaves
  Garlic
  Fresh root ginger

PREPARATION TIME *15 minutes*

COOKING TIME *8 minutes*

SERVES 4–6

1½ lb (700 g) smoked chicken
1 lb (450 g) Chinese leaves
1½ tablespoons oil (preferably groundnut)
3 tablespoons coarsely chopped garlic
1 tablespoon coarsely chopped fresh root ginger
1 tablespoon dark soy sauce
1 tablespoon Chinese rice wine or dry sherry

With your fingers tear the meat from the bones of the chicken. Cut it into large shreds and set aside. Discard the bones. Coarsely chop the Chinese leaves.

Heat a wok or large frying-pan, then add the oil, garlic and ginger. Stir-fry the mixture for 10 seconds and add the Chinese leaves. Continue to stir-fry for 5 minutes, add the soy sauce and rice wine and cook for another minute. Then add the smoked chicken and cook through. Serve at once.

CRISPY CHICKEN IN GARLIC-GINGER SAUCE

*H*ere is a dish that is quick and easy and still combines most of the qualities which make Chinese food so appealing: contrasting tastes and
textures; dipping sauces; crisp outside, tender inside; lightness and the
ability to satisfy at the same time. Most of the work is in the preparation,
with just a few minutes' cooking time – in fact you can prepare the chicken
and sauce several hours before you are ready to cook. Serve this as a main
course with rice and a simple salad.

SHOPPING LIST
1½ lb (700 g) chicken thighs
Spring onions
Garlic
Fresh root ginger

PREPARATION TIME *20 minutes*

COOKING TIME *7 minutes*

SERVES 4–6

1½ lb (700 g) chicken thighs
2 tablespoons light soy sauce
2 tablespoons Chinese rice
    wine or dry sherry
3 tablespoons coarsely chopped
    spring onions
2 tablespoons coarsely chopped
    garlic
1 tablespoon coarsely chopped
    fresh root ginger
15 fl oz (400 ml) oil
Cornflour for dusting
For the sauce
1 tablespoon light soy sauce
1 tablespoon sugar
1 tablespoon white rice vinegar
2 teaspoons sesame oil

Bone the chicken thighs by running a knife through to the bone
along their length, then opening each side of the meat, exposing the bone.
Combine the chicken with the soy sauce and rice wine.

Combine the spring onions, garlic and ginger in one bowl and
combine the sauce ingredients in another.

Heat a wok or large frying-pan, then add the oil (preferably
groundnut). Dust the chicken pieces with the cornflour and deep-fry for 5

minutes or until golden-brown. Remove from the wok and drain on kitchen paper, then place on a serving platter and keep warm. Drain all the oil from the wok and re-heat it. Add the spring onions, garlic and ginger and stir-fry for 20 seconds. Pour in the sauce ingredients and cook for a further 20 seconds. Serve the chicken with the sauce on the side.

RED-COOKED CHICKEN WINGS

'Red-cooking' simply means simmering in a richly flavoured sauce that also imparts a deep red colour to the food. Here I use chicken wings, the tastiest and most under-rated part of the bird – and the result is a tempting dish, nicely re-heatable and quick to make, taking only about 30 minutes. You can use chicken thighs and drumsticks instead of wings if you wish, but they will need a slightly longer cooking time.

SHOPPING LIST
1½ lb (700 g) chicken wings
Fresh root ginger
Garlic

PREPARATION TIME *14 minutes*

COOKING TIME *15 minutes*

SERVES 4–6

1½ lb (700 g) chicken wings
1 tablespoon oil (preferably groundnut)
1 tablespoon coarsely chopped fresh root ginger
1 tablespoon coarsely chopped garlic
½ teaspoon salt
2 tablespoons dark soy sauce
1 tablespoon Chinese rice wine or dry sherry
3 tablespoons hoisin sauce
2 teaspoons sugar
2 teaspoons chilli bean sauce
5 fl oz (150 ml) water

Cut the chicken wings in half at the joint.

Heat a wok or large frying-pan, then add the oil, ginger, garlic, and salt. Stir-fry the mixture for 10 seconds. Add all the other ingredients except the wings and simmer for 1 minute. Put in the wings, cover the wok and cook for 15 minutes or until the wings are cooked through. Serve at once or allow to cool and serve at room temperature.

Stir-Fried Chicken Livers with Onions

Chicken livers are among the easiest foods to prepare. The trick is to combine them with the proper seasonings and spices so that their delicateness is retained but they are also given a new dimension. Hence the onions and the five-spice powder in this recipe – and it works! Serve this dish as part of a Chinese meal or as a main course with rice and a vegetable. Calf's liver may be substituted for the chicken livers if you wish.

Shopping List
1 lb (450 g) chicken livers
2 onions

Preparation Time *14 minutes*

Cooking Time *11 minutes*

Serves 2–4

1 lb (450 g) chicken livers
1 tablespoon plus 2 teaspoons Chinese rice wine or dry sherry
1 tablespoon light soy sauce
½ teaspoon five-spice powder
1 teaspoon salt
¼ teaspoon freshly ground black pepper
1 tablespoon cornflour
2 teaspoons plus 1 tablespoon oil (preferably groundnut)
2 onions, peeled and sliced
2 teaspoons sesame oil

Cut the chicken livers into bite-sized pieces. Combine the livers with 1 tablespoon of the rice wine, the soy sauce, five-spice powder, ½ teaspoon of the salt, the pepper and cornflour. Mix well.

Heat a wok or large frying-pan, then add 2 teaspoons of the oil. Stir-fry the livers for about 4 minutes or until they are brown on the outside but still pink inside. Remove the livers from the wok. Wipe the wok clean, then re-heat. Add the remaining 1 tablespoon oil, ½ teaspoon salt and the onions. Stir-fry for 4 minutes or until the onions are brown and slightly caramelised. Return the livers to the wok and add the remaining 2 teaspoons rice wine and the sesame oil. Stir-fry for 2 more minutes. Serve at once.

BRAISED CHICKEN AND MUSHROOM CASSEROLE

*Y*es, clearly this takes a little longer than the average quick and easy meal but it is one of my mother's favourites and it *is* delicious. I recall my mother making it on winter mornings before she left for work, placing it with rice on the heater to keep warm so I could eat it for lunch.

SHOPPING LIST
1½ lb (700 g) chicken thighs
8 oz (225 g) onions
Garlic
Fresh root ginger

PREPARATION TIME *23 minutes*

COOKING TIME *11 minutes*

SERVES 4–6

1 oz (25 g) Chinese dried mushrooms
1½ pints (900 ml) warm water
1½ lb (700 g) chicken thighs
1 tablespoon oil (preferably groundnut)
8 oz (225 g) onions, peeled and sliced
2 tablespoons coarsely chopped garlic
1 tablespoon coarsely chopped fresh root ginger
2 tablespoons Chinese rice wine or dry sherry
4 tablespoons oyster sauce

Soak the dried mushrooms in the warm water for 20 minutes until soft. While the mushrooms are soaking, remove the skin and bones from the chicken thighs and discard. Cut the flesh into 1 inch (2.5 cm) cubes. Prepare the rest of the ingredients.

Squeeze the excess liquid from the mushrooms and remove and discard the stalks. Cut the caps into quarters. Save the soaking liquid.

Heat a wok or large frying-pan, then add the oil and chicken. Stir-fry for 3½ minutes or until the chicken begins to brown. Pour off any excess fat, re-heat the wok, add the onions, garlic, ginger and mushrooms and stir-fry for 2 minutes. Then add 5 fl oz (150 ml) of the liquid in which the mushrooms were soaked, the rice wine and oyster sauce. Continue cooking over high heat for 5 minutes. Serve at once.

Orange-lemon Chicken

Orange and lemon are wonderful flavours that chicken breasts readily absorb and blend with. This is a classic quick and easy meal, quite satisfying as a main course with plain rice and a salad. Alternatively, serve it at room temperature as part of a cold buffet or as exotic picnic fare.

SHOPPING LIST

12 oz (350 g) boneless
  chicken breasts
Garlic
Fresh root ginger
1 orange
1 lemon
Spring onions

PREPARATION TIME *15 minutes*

COOKING TIME *5 minutes*

SERVES 2

12 oz (350 g) boneless chicken breasts
Salt
1 tablespoon oil (preferably
  groundnut)
2 tablespoons coarsely chopped garlic
1 teaspoon finely chopped fresh
  root ginger
2 teaspoons finely chopped
  orange rind
2 teaspoons finely chopped lemon rind
4 tablespoons orange juice
4 tablespoons lemon juice
1 tablespoon light soy sauce
1 tablespoon sugar
1 teaspoon cornflour mixed
  with 1 teaspoon water
1 teaspoon chilli bean sauce
2 teaspoons sesame oil
3 tablespoons coarsely chopped
  spring onions

Remove the skin from the chicken and cut the meat into long strips. Blanch the chicken for 30 seconds in a pan of boiling, salted water. Drain and set aside.

Heat a wok or large frying-pan, then add the oil, garlic and ginger. Stir-fry the mixture for 10 seconds and add the rest of the ingredients except for the chicken. Bring the mixture to a simmer, add the chicken to the wok and cook through. Remember that the chicken will continue to cook for at least 30 seconds after you have removed it from the wok, so be sure not to over-cook it. Serve at once.

STIR-FRIED TURKEY WITH PEPPERS

*H*ere again I substitute nutritious, low-fat turkey meat for chicken and it works wonderfully as a stir-fried meal. The red peppers add spice and colour to this wholesome and inexpensive dish, though you can success-fully substitute green peppers or even courgettes if these are not available.

SHOPPING LIST
1 lb (450 g) turkey breast
1 lb (450 g) red peppers

PREPARATION TIME *10 minutes*

COOKING TIME *4–5 minutes*

SERVES 2–4

1 lb (450 g) turkey breast
1 lb (450 g) red peppers
1½ tablespoons oil (preferably groundnut)
2 tablespoons Chinese rice wine or dry sherry
½ teaspoon salt
1 tablespoon oyster sauce

For the marinade
1½ tablespoons light soy sauce
1 tablespoon Chinese rice wine or dry sherry
2 teaspoons sesame oil
2 teaspoons cornflour

Cut the turkey breast into ½ × 3 inch (1 × 7.5 cm) cubes. Combine with the marinade ingredients in a medium-sized bowl and leave to stand for 5 minutes. De-seed the red peppers and cut them into ½ inch (1 cm) wide strips. Set aside.

Heat a wok or large frying-pan, then add the oil. Add the turkey and stir-fry for 10 seconds. Then add the pepper strips and stir-fry for another 10 seconds. Finally add the rice wine, salt, and oyster sauce and continue to stir-fry for 2–3 minutes. Remember that the turkey will conti-nue to cook for a short time after it is removed from the wok so under-cook rather than over-cook it and risk it becoming dry. Serve at once.

3

MEAT

*M*eat is a very popular food in China but it is not consumed in such quantities as in the West. That is, it is rarely the central dish in any meal. Rather, it is used to accompany and to complement other foods – vegetables and rice, for example – or in sauces and soups. This makes for a very healthy diet: in the West we use too much animal protein, at the cost of the vegetable nutrients and food fibre our bodies require.

The Chinese prepare meat in a number of basic ways: steaming, stir-frying, braising and frying are the techniques most often used. Meat is almost always cut into small pieces or thin slices. This makes for minimum cooking and maximum retention of natural flavours and juices. 'Quick and easy' is the general rule in China for the preparation of meat.

The recipes here may readily be offered as main courses. In some cases, which I note, the dishes can be made well ahead of time and

re-heated when needed. All of them are delectable and none is too complicated. I indicate which ones go well with rice and thus quite naturally can
be part of a one-dish meal, with perhaps a favourite salad.

FAST SPICY MEAT SAUCE FOR NOODLES

Simplicity itself, this marvellously tasty meat sauce transforms a lowly
plate of noodles into an impressive meal. If you expect a large crowd,
simply expand the recipe proportionately. The sauce freezes well, so you
could make several batches and freeze those you do not need
immediately. You can substitute minced beef for the pork if you wish. For
quick and successful informal entertaining, this dish cannot be beaten.

SHOPPING LIST
    Garlic
    Spring onions
    Fresh root ginger
    1 lb (450 g) minced pork

PREPARATION TIME *10–15 minutes*

COOKING TIME *8 minutes*

SERVES 4–6

1½ tablespoons oil
2 tablespoons coarsely chopped
    garlic
3 tablespoons coarsely chopped
    spring onions
2 tablespoons coarsely chopped
    fresh root ginger
1 lb (450 g) minced pork
1 tablespoon chilli bean sauce
1 tablespoon dark soy sauce
2 tablespoons Chinese rice
    wine or dry sherry
2 tablespoons hoisin sauce
1 teaspoon salt
2 teaspoons sugar

Heat a wok or large frying-pan, then add the oil. Add the garlic,
spring onions and ginger and stir-fry for 1 minute. Then add the pork and
stir-fry for 2 minutes. Add the chilli bean sauce, soy sauce, rice wine, hoisin sauce, salt and sugar and continue to cook for another 5 minutes.
Serve with noodles or over rice.

DO-AHEAD RE-HEATABLE BLACK BEAN SPARERIBS

*B*raised dishes make for quick and easy re-heating. They require a long cooking time in order to bring out their flavour, but once they have been cooked (which can be done even days ahead), the re-heating only improves it. I like to make this dish the night before, then let it cool, remove any fat, cover it and put it in the refrigerator; I then re-heat it when I get home. It also freezes extremely well. The dish is lovely on a cool day served with rice and vegetables.

SHOPPING LIST
> *2 lb (900 g) pork spareribs*
> *Spring onions*
> *Garlic*
> *Fresh root ginger*
> *8 oz (225 g) onions*

PREPARATION TIME *15 minutes*

COOKING TIME *50–55 minutes*

SERVES 4–6

2 lb (900 g) pork spareribs
1½ tablespoons oil (preferably groundnut)
3 tablespoons coarsely chopped black beans
3 tablespoons coarsely chopped spring onions
1½ tablespoons finely chopped garlic
1 tablespoon finely chopped fresh root ginger
8 oz (225 g) onions, sliced
5 fl oz (150 ml) Chinese rice wine or dry sherry
5 fl oz (150 ml) water
2 tablespoons dark soy sauce
2 tablespoons light soy sauce
2 teaspoons sugar
1 tablespoon sesame oil

Separate the spareribs into individual ribs and set aside.

Heat a wok or large frying-pan and add the oil. Brown the spareribs, then transfer them to a large heavy saucepan or flameproof casserole. Add the black beans, spring onions, garlic and ginger and stir-fry for 10 seconds. Put in the onions and continue to stir-fry for 2 minutes. Then add the rice wine, water, soy sauces and sugar. Bring the mixture to the boil. Pour this over the spareribs in the saucepan and simmer, covered, for 40 minutes or until the ribs are tender. Uncover and cook over a high heat for 5 minutes to reduce the sauce and finally stir in the sesame oil. Serve at once or allow to cool and re-heat when needed.

SAVOURY CUSTARD WITH PORK, SPRING ONIONS AND OYSTER SAUCE

*T*his sounds complicated but it is quite simple to prepare. Cracking the eggs and chopping the onions take the most time – 5 minutes. The minced meat cooks very quickly. As a child I watched my mother make this dish many times. Served with rice and vegetables, it is a fine, nutritious, family meal.

SHOPPING LIST
  6 eggs
  8 oz (225 g) minced pork
  Spring onions

PREPARATION TIME *12 minutes*

COOKING TIME *12 minutes*

SERVES 4–6

6 eggs, beaten
8 oz (225 g) minced pork
4 tablespoons coarsely chopped
  spring onions
1½ teaspoons salt
2 teaspoons light soy sauce
2 tablespoons oyster sauce
  mixed with 1 teaspoon water

Set a rack in a wok or deep pan. Put in water to a depth of 2½ inches (6 cm) and bring it to a simmer.

Combine the eggs, pork, spring onions, salt and soy sauce and mix well. Pour this into a heatproof dish and set the dish on the rack in the wok. Cover tightly and steam slowly for 12 minutes or until the custard has just set.

Remove the dish from the wok and drizzle with the oyster sauce mixture. Serve at once.

STIR-FRIED PORK WITH LITCHIS

*P*ork is the 'red meat' of China but, even so, it is almost always served as an accompaniment to other non-meat foods. In this recipe it is paired with litchi fruit. Try to use fresh litchis: their tangy, grape-like flavour goes nicely with that of pork, at once complementing and contrasting with it. Serve over rice.

SHOPPING LIST

1 lb (450 g) lean pork
8 oz (225 g) fresh or tinned
   litchis
Garlic
Spring onions

PREPARATION TIME *15 minutes (if using tinned litchis); 21 minutes (if using fresh litchis)*

COOKING TIME *3–4 minutes*

SERVES 4–6

1 lb (450 g) lean pork
2 teaspoons light soy sauce
2 teaspoons Chinese rice wine or dry sherry
1 teaspoon sesame oil
2 teaspoons cornflour
8 oz (225 g) fresh or tinned litchis
1½ tablespoons oil (preferably groundnut)
2 tablespoons coarsely chopped garlic
2 tablespoons coarsely chopped spring onions to garnish

Cut the pork into thick ¼ × 2 inch (0.5 × 5 cm) slices and put them into a bowl. Add the soy sauce, rice wine, sesame oil and cornflour and mix well.

If you are using fresh litchis, peel and de-seed them. Set aside. If you are using tinned litchis, drain off the liquid (which you will not need in this recipe) and set the fruit aside.

Heat a wok or large frying-pan, add the oil and garlic and stir-fry for 10 seconds. Put in the pork and continue to stir-fry for 1½ minutes or until it is just cooked through. Add the litchis and continue to stir-fry for another 30 seconds to warm them through. Garnish with the chopped spring onions and serve at once.

MANGO BEEF

*T*his is an example of the New Hong Kong Cuisine, and fast as well. Hong Kong chefs have adapted the exotic mango to new uses, as in this recipe. The soft texture and sensual sweetness of the fruit offer a wonderful contrast and complement to the sturdy familiar virtues of beef. Most of the work involved is preparatory; the cooking takes but a few minutes. Mango Beef is delicious and impressive enough to serve as a main course for either a family or a formal meal.

SHOPPING LIST
1 lb (450 g) lean beef steak
2 fresh mangoes

PREPARATION TIME *15 minutes*

COOKING TIME *3–4 minutes*

SERVES 4–6

1 lb (450 g) lean beef steak
1 tablespoon plus 1 teaspoon
    light soy sauce
3 teaspoons Chinese rice wine
    or dry sherry
2 teaspoons cornflour
2 fresh mangoes
1½ tablespoons oil (preferably
    groundnut)
2 teaspoons dark soy sauce

Cut the beef into thick ¼ × 2 inch (0.5 × 5 cm) slices and put them into a bowl. Add 1 tablespoon of the light soy sauce, 2 teaspoons of the rice wine and the cornflour and mix well.

Peel the mangoes and cut them into thick slices, discarding the stones.

Heat a wok or large frying-pan, then pour in the oil. Add the beef and stir-fry for 2 minutes to brown. Add the remaining 1 teaspoon light soy sauce, the dark soy sauce and the remaining 1 teaspoon rice wine and stir-fry for 30 seconds. Then add the mango slices and heat them through. Give the mixture a final stir and serve at once. The beef should be slightly undercooked as it continues to cook for a short time after it is removed from the wok.

CHINESE LAMB CURRY

*L*amb is typically a northern Chinese food but the ingenious chefs of the south have taken it and blended it with a familiar Southeast Asian seasoning, curry. This combination appeals to the Southern Chinese palate: curry is a familiar seasoning and assertive enough to mask the strong taste of the lamb, a taste that most Chinese do not particularly relish.

Chinese Lamb Curry is excellent for entertaining because it can be prepared ahead of time and simply re-heated when needed – and it is even tastier then. If you wish, you can prepare the dish in advance up to the point at which the vegetables are added and complete it, cooking the vegetables, just before you are ready to serve. It goes well with rice and perhaps a salad.

SHOPPING LIST
2½ lb (1.25 kg) breast of lamb
Garlic
Fresh root ginger
1 lb (450 g) potatoes
8 oz (225 g) carrots

PREPARATION TIME *18 minutes*

COOKING TIME *45 minutes*

SERVES 4–6

2½ lb (1.25 kg) breast of lamb
1½ tablespoons oil (preferably groundnut)
2 tablespoons coarsely chopped garlic
1 tablespoon coarsely chopped fresh root ginger
1 pint (570 ml) water
3 tablespoons light soy sauce
2 tablespoons dark soy sauce
6 tablespoons Madras curry paste or powder
1 tablespoon sugar
1 lb (450 g) potatoes
8 oz (225 g) carrots

Cut the lamb meat from the bone and then cube it. Blanch it in boiling water for 10 minutes. Drain and place in a flameproof casserole.

Heat a wok or large frying-pan, then add the oil, garlic and ginger and stir-fry for 10 seconds. Add the water, soy sauces, curry paste or powder and sugar and bring the mixture to the boil. Pour the liquid over the lamb in the casserole and bring to the boil again. Cover and simmer for 35 minutes or until the meat is tender.

Peel the potatoes and cut them into 1 inch (2.5 cm) cubes. Peel the carrots and cut them into 1 inch (2.5 cm) lengths. Skim the fat from the curry and add the vegetables. Cook for another 10 minutes or until the vegetables are tender, then serve.

TOMATO BEEF WITH ONIONS

I learned to make this quick and easy dish in my uncle's restaurant. I still make it when tomatoes are in season. It is a wonderful combination of two good foods, bound together by the richness of the seasonings and the oyster sauce. Serve it over egg noodles or plain rice.

SHOPPING LIST

1 lb (450 g) lean beef steak
8 oz (225 g) onions
1 lb (450 g) tomatoes

PREPARATION TIME *15 minutes*

COOKING TIME *10 minutes*

SERVES 4–6

1 lb (450 g) lean beef steak
1 tablespoon light soy sauce
2 teaspoons Chinese rice wine
    or dry sherry
2 teaspoons cornflour
8 oz (225 g) onions
1 lb (450 g) tomatoes
2 tablespoons oil (preferably
    groundnut)
2 tablespoons water
3 tablespoons oyster sauce

Cut the beef into thick ¼ × 2 inch (0.5 × 5 cm) slices and put them into a bowl. Add the soy sauce, rice wine and cornflour and mix well.

Peel the onions and cut into thick slices. Quarter the tomatoes.

Heat a wok or large frying-pan, then pour in the oil. Add the beef and stir-fry for 2 minutes to brown. Remove the beef with a slotted spoon and set aside. Add the onions to the wok and stir-fry for 1 minute. Pour in the water and cook for 3 minutes. Drain the juices from the beef into the wok. Continue to cook for another 2 minutes. Add the tomatoes and oyster sauce and cook until the tomatoes are just heated through (they should not be allowed to become mushy). Return the beef to the wok, heat through and serve at once.

Hot and Tangy Minced Lamb

*L*amb has a very assertive taste even when it is minced; thus we can use hot and tangy sauces with it and its flavour is still recognisable but in a more palatable form. As is the case with meat sauces in general, this lamb dish, in which the flavours of East and West meet, readily combines with pasta, rice, noodles or even bread to make a quick, easy and substantial meal for four to six people in less than 30 minutes. You can use minced beef instead of lamb if you wish.

SHOPPING LIST
- *1 lb (450 g) minced lamb*
- *Garlic*
- *Fresh root ginger*
- *1 lemon*

PREPARATION TIME *15 minutes*

COOKING TIME *8 minutes*

SERVES 4–6

- 1 tablespoon oil (preferably groundnut)
- 1 lb (450 g) minced lamb
- 3 tablespoons coarsely chopped garlic
- 2 tablespoons coarsely chopped fresh root ginger
- 2 tablespoons tomato purée
- 2 tablespoons sesame paste
- 1½ tablespoons dark soy sauce
- 1 tablespoon lemon juice
- 1 tablespoon chilli bean sauce
- 2 teaspoons sugar
- 1 tablespoon Chinese rice wine or dry sherry

Heat a wok or large frying-pan, then add the oil and lamb. Stir-fry for 2 minutes and add the garlic and ginger. Continue cooking for another minute, then stir in the tomato purée, sesame paste, soy sauce, lemon juice, chilli bean sauce, sugar and rice wine. (You will find it quicker, when required to add a number of ingredients at the same time as here, to measure them all into one bowl and add them in one go.) Cook for another 4 minutes. Serve at once.

4

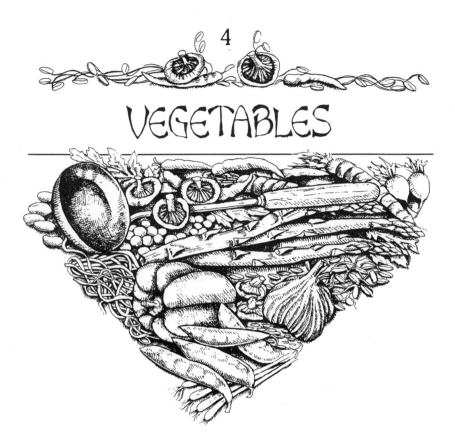

VEGETABLES

Of all the foods we normally cook, vegetables are undoubtedly the quickest and easiest to prepare. They are generally delicate in flavour and cook rapidly. Thus we need to take great care that we cook them to just the right point or risk losing their natural taste, juice, colour, texture and food value. Properly cooked, vegetables are very nutritious and an extremely important part of the diet.

The Chinese are masters of the art of vegetable cooking, and stir-frying is the perfect technique for vegetables. This rapid method of cooking over high heat retains all of the virtues of the food and leaves it neither raw nor mushy: it is a pleasure to eat. Almost all vegetables may be stir-fried, as the recipes here indicate. Follow them but adapt them to your own taste. Use vegetables in season imaginatively and creatively.

RED-COOKED WINTER VEGETABLES

*R*ed-cooking is usually reserved for meats – simmering them in a rich red sauce of Chinese spices. The technique works as well, however, with winter root vegetables, making a quick tasty stew. On a cold winter evening, this dish goes perfectly with meat or poultry and a salad.

SHOPPING LIST
1 lb (450 g) carrots
8 oz (225 g) turnips
Garlic
Fresh root ginger

PREPARATION TIME *10 minutes*

COOKING TIME *12 minutes*

SERVES 4

1 lb (450 g) carrots
8 oz (225 g) turnips
1 tablespoon oil (preferably groundnut)
2 cloves garlic, peeled and crushed
2 teaspoons coarsely chopped fresh root ginger
3 tablespoons hoisin sauce
1 tablespoon dark soy sauce
2 teaspoons sugar
5 fl oz (150 ml) water

Peel and cut the carrots into 1 inch (2.5 cm) pieces. Peel the turnips and cut them into 1 inch (2.5 cm) cubes.

Heat a wok or large frying-pan, then add the oil, garlic and ginger. Stir-fry for 10 seconds and add the carrots, hoisin sauce, soy sauce, sugar and water. Cover and cook over a high heat for 8 minutes. Then add the turnips and continue to cook for another 3 minutes or until all the vegetables are tender. There should be very little sauce left. Turn on to a platter and serve at once.

STIR-FRIED EGGS AND CORN WITH SPRING ONIONS AND GINGER

I often make this dish when I am hungry and need a sustaining nutritious meal in a hurry. Corn has made its way from the West to China, and in Hong Kong especially you will find it a popular food. As this delicious combination indicates, Chinese chefs have thoroughly integrated corn into the Chinese cuisine. You can substitute fresh or frozen peas for the corn if you wish.

SHOPPING LIST
1 lb (450 g) fresh sweetcorn on the cob or 10 oz (275 g) frozen sweetcorn
Spring onions
Fresh root ginger
4 eggs

PREPARATION TIME *10 minutes*

COOKING TIME *5 minutes*

SERVES 4

1 lb (450 g) fresh sweetcorn on the cob or 10 oz (275 g) frozen sweetcorn
1 tablespoon oil (preferably groundnut)
3 tablespoons coarsely chopped spring onions
2 teaspoons finely chopped fresh root ginger
1 teaspoon salt
4 eggs, lightly beaten

If you are using fresh corn on the cob, clean it and remove the kernels with a sharp knife or cleaver – you should end up with about 10 oz (275 g). Set it aside. If you are using frozen corn, place it in a bowl and let it thaw at room temperature.

Heat a wok or large frying-pan, then add the oil. Add the spring onions, ginger and salt and stir-fry for 10 seconds. Add the corn and continue to stir-fry for 2 minutes. Finally, turn the heat to medium, add the eggs and continue to cook for another 2 minutes. Serve at once.

STIR-FRIED PEAS WITH FRESH CORIANDER AND SPRING ONIONS

*B*ecause of their sweetness and succulent texture, peas are always popular. Here I have enhanced their virtues with some spirited seasonings to make a quick, easy and tasty vegetable dish. Try also serving it at room temperature as part of a buffet.

SHOPPING LIST
> *1 lb (450 g) fresh peas (shelled weight) or frozen peas*
> *Fresh coriander*
> *Spring onions*
> *Garlic*

PREPARATION TIME *11 minutes (if using fresh peas); 5 minutes (if using frozen peas)*

COOKING TIME *4 minutes*

SERVES 4–6

1 lb (450 g) fresh peas (shelled weight) or frozen peas
1 tablespoon oil (preferably groundnut)
2 tablespoons finely chopped fresh coriander
2 tablespoons finely chopped spring onions
2 teaspoons finely chopped garlic
1 teaspoon sugar
1 teaspoon salt
½ teaspoon freshly ground white pepper
2 teaspoons sesame oil

If you are using fresh peas, blanch them in boiling water for 2 minutes, drain and set aside. If you are using frozen peas, let them thaw at room temperature.

Heat a wok or large frying-pan, then add the oil. Add the peas and stir-fry for 30 seconds, then add the coriander, spring onions, garlic, sugar, salt and pepper and continue to stir-fry for 3 minutes or until the peas are cooked. Add the sesame oil, give the mixture a final stir and serve at once.

POTATOES IN
CURRY-COCONUT STEW

*T*his is essentially a potato stew, but one given new dimensions by the savoury and exotic seasonings. Moreover, it is ready in little more than 30 minutes, and if it is more convenient you can peel the potatoes up to 4 hours in advance and leave them, covered with water, in the refrigerator until you want to cook them. You can also substitute carrots or turnips for the potatoes. The rich flavour and substantial nature of this dish make for a very satisfying vegetarian meal. Serve it with a green vegetable or salad.

SHOPPING LIST
> *1½ lb (700 g) potatoes*
> *8 oz (225 g) onions*
> *Garlic*
> *Fresh root ginger*

PREPARATION TIME *19 minutes*

COOKING TIME *17 minutes*

SERVES 4–6

1½ lb (700 g) potatoes
8 oz (225 g) onions
1½ tablespoons oil (preferably groundnut)
2 tablespoons coarsely chopped garlic
1 tablespoon coarsely chopped fresh root ginger
3 tablespoons curry paste
15 fl oz (400 ml) tinned coconut milk
4 tablespoons water
1 tablespoon light soy sauce
2 teaspoons sugar

Peel the potatoes and cut them into 1 inch (2.5 cm) cubes. Peel and coarsely chop the onions.

Heat a wok or large frying-pan, then add the oil, onions, garlic and ginger. Stir-fry the mixture for 1 minute. Then add the potatoes, curry paste, coconut milk, water, soy sauce and sugar. Bring the mixture to a simmer, cover and cook for 15 minutes or until the potatoes are tender. Serve at once.

OYSTER SAUCE BEAN CURD

Bean curd (*tofu*) is an inexpensive, very nutritious food that is also delicious when combined with appropriate seasonings and properly cooked. Here oyster sauce and pan-frying create a most enjoyable bean curd dish.

SHOPPING LIST
1 lb (450 g) firm bean curd
Garlic

PREPARATION TIME *9 minutes*

COOKING TIME *12 minutes*

SERVES 4

1 lb (450 g) firm bean curd
3 tablespoons oil (preferably groundnut)
2 cloves garlic, peeled and crushed
3 tablespoons oyster sauce
2 tablespoons water
1 teaspoon sugar
2 teaspoons sesame oil

Cut the bean curd into 1 inch (2.5 cm) cubes.

Heat a wok or large frying-pan, then add the oil. Slowly fry the bean curd on each side until it is golden-brown – you may have to do this in several batches. Remove it from the wok and drain on kitchen paper.

Pour off from the wok all but 1 tablespoon of oil. Re-heat the wok and remaining oil, add the garlic and stir-fry for 10 seconds. Then add the oyster sauce, water, sugar and sesame oil. Bring to a simmer, return the bean curd cubes to the wok and heat them through. Serve at once.

FAST MANGE-TOUT WITH MUSHROOMS

These mange-tout (or Chinese peas, as they are sometimes called) are refreshingly different in that the crisp edible pod is so tasty a complement to the green peas themselves – they are among my very favourite vegetables, and so quick and easy to prepare. Combined with the softer, meatier mushrooms and enhancing seasonings, they make a splendid vegetable dish in less than 20 minutes.

SHOPPING LIST
8 oz (225 g) small mushrooms
1 lb (450 g) mange-tout

PREPARATION TIME *10 minutes*

COOKING TIME *7 minutes*

SERVES 4–6

1½ tablespoons oil (preferably groundnut)
8 oz (225 g) small mushrooms, wiped
1 lb (450 g) mange-tout, trimmed
1 teaspoon sugar
2 teaspoons dark soy sauce
2 teaspoons sesame oil

Heat a wok or large frying-pan and add the oil and mushrooms. Stir-fry for 4 minutes, then add the mange-tout, sugar, soy sauce and sesame oil. Continue to stir-fry for another 2 minutes. Serve at once.

STIR-FRIED GINGER SPINACH

The hardest part of this recipe is cleaning the spinach. After that, it is quick, easy and ginger-delicious all the way!

SHOPPING LIST
1½ lb (700 g) fresh spinach
Fresh root ginger

PREPARATION TIME *7 minutes*

COOKING TIME *5 minutes*

SERVES 4–6

1½ lb (700 g) fresh spinach
1 tablespoon oil (preferably groundnut)
2 tablespoons finely shredded fresh root ginger
1 teaspoon salt
1 teaspoon sugar
2 teaspoons sesame oil

Remove the stalks from the spinach leaves. Wash the leaves well in several changes of cold water.

Heat a wok or large frying-pan, then add the oil, ginger and salt. Stir-fry the mixture for 20 seconds. Add the spinach and stir-fry for 2 minutes to coat the leaves thoroughly with the mixture. When the spinach has wilted to about a third of its original size, add the sugar and sesame oil. Continue to stir-fry for another 2 minutes. Serve hot or cold.

BRIGHT PEPPER AND GREEN BEAN STIR-FRY

Red peppers and green beans, nicely seasoned, combine to form a colourful blend of tastes and textures, a nutritious and attractive salad appropriate for any meal: very quick, very easy and very satisfying. This dish is also good served at room temperature.

SHOPPING LIST
8 oz (225 g) red peppers
Garlic
8 oz (225 g) French beans

PREPARATION TIME *15 minutes*

COOKING TIME *7 minutes*

SERVES 4–6

8 oz (225 g) red peppers
1½ tablespoons oil (preferably groundnut)
2 tablespoons coarsely chopped garlic
1½ teaspoons salt
8 oz (225 g) French beans, trimmed and left whole
1 teaspoon sugar
2 tablespoons water

De-seed the peppers and cut them into strips.

Heat a wok or large frying-pan, then add the oil. Add the garlic, salt, peppers and beans and stir-fry for 2 minutes. Then add the sugar and water and continue to cook for another 4 minutes or until the vegetables are tender. Serve at once.

5

ΠΟΟDLES & RICE

*N*oodles are among the quickest foods to cook, and rice, while it takes a little longer, re-heats nicely and so can be prepared in advance. Indeed, some rice dishes require re-heated rice. Asian cities are filled with street stalls and wagons that sell the area's 'fast food', rice and noodles, for a quick meal or snack. These are warming and satisfying dishes, easy to serve and as easy to make. They are the perfect base for a one-dish meal.

Some of the preparation for a rice dish can be done ahead of time, and once the rice is made the rest of the dish is rapidly put together. In most of the noodle recipes I use rice noodles for convenience. These keep indefinitely in their dried state, needing no refrigeration. They require very little cooking – not even the short boiling that egg noodles and pasta need – and can be placed directly into the dish being prepared. If time is really at a premium, rely on rice noodles.

Many of the dishes in this section may serve as part of a larger meal or simply as a light meal in themselves – rice and pasta are quite satisfying. Some of the recipes can be served at room temperature for a buffet or as exotic picnic fare. Use them creatively and imaginatively, to suit your own taste and needs.

QUICK FRIED RICE

*I*f you prepare the rice beforehand, this dish takes but 16 minutes from wok to table. You can boil the rice hours or even days in advance and store it, well covered, in the refrigerator. This recipe is typical of the fried rice served in Chinese homes, with just a few simple seasonings to perk up the bland but congenial cereal. Serve it as part of a meal with a fast meat or poultry dish and your favourite salad. Alternatively, turn Quick Fried Rice into a speedy one-dish meal by adding left-overs.

SHOPPING LIST
> *Fresh root ginger*
> *4 eggs*

PREPARATION TIME *rice – 5 minutes;*
> *Quick Fried Rice – 8 minutes*

COOKING TIME *rice – 25 minutes;*
> *Quick Fried Rice – 7–8 minutes*

SERVES 4–6

15 fl oz (400 ml) long-grain rice
1½ pints (900 ml) water
2 tablespoons oil (preferably groundnut)
2 teaspoons salt
2 tablespoons coarsely chopped fresh root ginger
4 eggs, beaten

Put the rice in a heavy pan with the water and bring it to the boil. Continue boiling for about 10 minutes or until most of the surface liquid has evaporated. The surface of the rice should have small indentations and look rather like a pitted crater. At this point cover the pan with a very tight-fitting lid, turn the heat as low as possible and let the rice cook undisturbed for 15 minutes more. Remove from the heat and allow to cool thoroughly.

Heat a wok or large frying-pan, add the oil, salt and ginger and stir-fry for 1 minute. Now add the cooked rice and continue to stir-fry for another 5 minutes. Stir in the eggs and cook for 1 minute. Serve at once or allow to cool and serve at room temperature.

HOT AND SPICY RICE WITH BEEF

*R*ice dishes need not be bland, as the aromatic seasonings and spices in this recipe prove. This can be a one-dish meal; simply serve it with a favourite salad or vegetable. Speed up the preparation by boiling the rice in advance – store it, well covered, in the refrigerator until you need it.

SHOPPING LIST
1 lb (450 g) minced beef
Garlic
Fresh root ginger
Spring onions

PREPARATION TIME *rice – 5 minutes;*
Hot and Spicy Rice – 7 minutes

COOKING TIME *rice – 25 minutes;*
Hot and Spicy Rice – 10 minutes

SERVES 4–6

15 fl oz (400 ml) long-grain rice
1½ pints (900 ml) water
4 tablespoons oil (preferably
  groundnut)
2 teaspoons salt
1 lb (450 g) minced beef
2 tablespoons coarsely chopped
  garlic
1 tablespoon coarsely chopped
  fresh root ginger
2 teaspoons chilli bean sauce
1 teaspoon curry paste or
  powder
3 tablespoons coarsely chopped
  spring onions

Put the rice in a heavy pan with the water and bring it to the boil. Continue boiling for about 10 minutes or until most of the surface liquid has evaporated. The surface of the rice should have small indentations and look rather like a pitted crater. At this point, cover the pan with a very tight-fitting lid, turn the heat as low as possible and let the rice cook undisturbed for 15 minutes more. Remove from the heat and allow to cool.

Heat a wok or large frying-pan and add 2 tablespoons of the oil and the salt. Add the beef and stir-fry for 4 minutes, stirring well to break up any clumps of meat. Remove the cooked meat from the wok and set aside. Drain the oil from the wok. Re-heat the wok and add the remaining 2 tablespoons oil. Then add the garlic, ginger, chilli bean sauce and curry paste or powder and stir-fry for 30 seconds. Now add the cooked rice and beef and the spring onions and continue to stir-fry for another 5 minutes. Serve at once or allow to cool and serve at room temperature.

RICE NOODLES WITH BROCCOLI

*T*his recipe takes advantage of the quick cooking characteristics of rice noodles. Boiled for about 2 minutes and then combined with the blanched broccoli for another few minutes, the noodles make a delectable vegetarian dish for one or two people. For a more spicy flavour add 2 teaspoons chilli bean sauce when you add the other sauces. Any left-overs can be re-heated very easily by stir-frying.

SHOPPING LIST

1 lb (450 g) broccoli
12 oz (350 g) thin dried rice noodles
Garlic
Spring onions

PREPARATION TIME *15 minutes*

COOKING TIME *8 minutes*

SERVES 4–6

Salt
1 lb (450 g) broccoli
12 oz (350 g) thin dried rice noodles
1½ tablespoons oil (preferably groundnut)
2 tablespoons coarsely chopped garlic
2 tablespoons coarsely chopped spring onions
3 tablespoons water
2 tablespoons oyster sauce
1 tablespoon dark soy sauce
2 teaspoons sesame oil

Fill a large pan with water, add salt to taste and bring to the boil. Separate the broccoli heads into small florets, and peel and slice the stems. Blanch the broccoli pieces in the boiling water for 4 minutes.

Place the rice noodles in a large heatproof bowl. Drain the hot water from the blanched broccoli over the rice noodles and immerse the broccoli pieces in cold water. Drain the broccoli thoroughly and set aside.

Let the noodles stand in the hot water for 2 minutes, then drain. Heat a wok or large frying-pan and add the oil, garlic and spring onions. Stir-fry for 20 seconds. Stir in the drained rice noodles and broccoli and continue to stir-fry for 1 minute. Then add the water, oyster sauce, soy sauce and sesame oil and cook for 2 minutes. Turn the mixture on to a platter and serve at once.

SPICY RICE NOODLES WITH MUSSELS

*T*his dish is useful for entertaining a large group of friends at short notice. Only the careful cleaning of the mussels takes any time; the rest of the preparation is very quick. Make sure that all the mussels are firmly closed before cooking: throw away any that do not close up when touched or that have damaged shells. You can substitute prawns or clams for mussels, but whatever seafood you use will result in a tasty and substantial dish that, with rice noodles, for example, makes a complete and satisfying meal.

SHOPPING LIST
    Garlic
    Spring onions
    2 lb (900 g) fresh mussels

PREPARATION TIME *23 minutes*

COOKING TIME *8–9 minutes plus 15 minutes' standing time*

SERVES 4–6

8 oz (225 g) rice noodles, rice vermicelli or rice sticks
2 tablespoons oil (preferably groundnut)
1 tablespoon black beans
2 tablespoons coarsely chopped garlic
2 tablespoons coarsely chopped spring onions
2 lb (900 g) fresh mussels, well scrubbed
1 tablespoon Chinese rice wine or dry sherry
1 tablespoon yellow bean sauce
2 teaspoons chilli bean sauce

Bring a large saucepan of water to the boil, remove from heat and add the rice noodles. Leave to stand for about 15 minutes, then drain well.
    Heat a wok or large frying-pan and add the oil, black beans (leave these whole), garlic and spring onions. Stir-fry for 20 seconds and add the mussels, rice wine, yellow bean sauce and chilli bean sauce. Continue to cook for 5 minutes or until all the mussels have opened. Discard any which have not opened. Add the rice noodles and cook for another 2 minutes, mixing well. Give the dish a final stir and serve at once.

ELIZABETH CHONG'S NOODLE SALAD

As one of Australia's leading teachers of Chinese cookery, Elizabeth Chong is very much worth listening to. And because she leads so busy a professional life – teaching, travelling, demonstrating and writing – she is an authority on quick, easy and delicious meals. This recipe, which I have adapted from one of her own, represents the best of good food, even though it is so simple to prepare. Serve the salad on a bed of lettuce surrounded with sliced tomatoes as an unusual side dish – most refreshing on a warm day!

SHOPPING LIST
12 oz (350 g) bean sprouts
Spring onions

PREPARATION TIME *15 minutes*

COOKING TIME *2 minutes*

SERVES 4–6

6 oz (175 g) bean thread noodles
1 tablespoon oil (preferably groundnut)
2 teaspoons salt
12 oz (350 g) bean sprouts
6 spring onions, finely shredded
1½ teaspoons chilli bean sauce
1½ tablespoons white rice vinegar
1 tablespoon light soy sauce
2 teaspoons sesame oil

Soak the noodles in a large bowl of warm water for 5 minutes. (While they are soaking, prepare the other ingredients.) When the noodles are soft, drain them well and cut them into 3 inch (7.5 cm) lengths using scissors or a knife.

Heat a wok or large frying-pan and add the oil, salt, bean sprouts and spring onions. Stir-fry for 10 seconds, then add the chilli bean sauce, rice vinegar, soy sauce, sesame oil and noodles and cook for 1 minute. Allow the mixture to cool, then refrigerate. Serve cold as an accompaniment to grilled or cold meats.

INDEX